50 French Tea-Time Treats

By: Kelly Johnson

Table of Contents

- Madeleines
- Croissants
- Financiers
- Éclairs
- Tarte Tatin
- Macarons
- Pain au chocolat
- Brioche
- Clafoutis
- Chouquettes
- Canelés
- Gougères
- Tarte au citron
- Gâteau Basque
- Paris-Brest
- Opéra cake
- Palmiers
- Parisian flan
- Mont-Blanc
- Mille-feuille
- Bûche de Noël
- Madeleines de Commercy
- Quatre-quarts
- Gâteau de Mamie
- Pithiviers
- Financier au chocolat
- Crêpes Suzette
- Mousse au chocolat
- Poached pears in red wine
- Tartelette aux fruits
- Choux à la crème
- Sablés
- Tarte Bourdaloue
- Caramelized apple cake
- Gâteau Saint-Honoré

- Pain d'épices
- Dacquoise
- Parisian macarons with fruit filling
- Flan pâtissier
- Gâteau au yaourt
- Tartelette au chocolat
- Framboisier
- Palet breton
- Crêpes with sugar
- Nougat
- Meringues
- Biscuit rose de Reims
- Tarte normande
- Gâteau de voyage
- Sablé Breton

Madeleines

Ingredients:

- 1 cup (125g) all-purpose flour
- 1/2 tsp baking powder
- 1/4 tsp salt
- 1/2 cup (115g) unsalted butter, melted
- 1/2 cup (100g) granulated sugar
- 2 large eggs
- 1 tsp vanilla extract
- Zest of 1 lemon (optional)

Instructions:

1. Preheat oven to 375°F (190°C) and grease a madeleine pan.
2. In a bowl, whisk together flour, baking powder, and salt.
3. Beat eggs and sugar until light and fluffy. Stir in melted butter, vanilla, and lemon zest.
4. Gradually add dry ingredients and mix until just combined.
5. Spoon the batter into the madeleine molds, filling each about 3/4 full.
6. Bake for 10-12 minutes until golden. Let cool in the pan for a few minutes before transferring to a wire rack.

Croissants

Ingredients:

- 4 cups (500g) all-purpose flour
- 1/4 cup (50g) granulated sugar
- 1 tsp salt
- 1 packet (7g) active dry yeast
- 1 1/2 cups (360ml) cold milk
- 2 tbsp unsalted butter, softened
- 1 1/4 cups (285g) cold unsalted butter, cubed

Instructions:

1. Dissolve yeast and sugar in warm milk, let sit for 5-10 minutes.
2. Mix flour and salt in a bowl, add yeast mixture, and knead into a dough.
3. Chill dough for 30 minutes, then roll into a rectangle. Place cold butter in the center and fold dough over it.
4. Roll dough into a long rectangle, fold into thirds, then refrigerate for 30 minutes. Repeat this process 3-4 times.
5. Roll out dough and cut into triangles. Roll each triangle tightly and form into croissants.
6. Let rise for 1-2 hours, then bake at 400°F (200°C) for 12-15 minutes until golden brown.

Financiers

Ingredients:

- 1/2 cup (115g) unsalted butter
- 1 cup (120g) almond flour
- 1/2 cup (60g) all-purpose flour
- 1/2 cup (100g) granulated sugar
- 1/4 tsp salt
- 4 large egg whites
- 1 tsp vanilla extract

Instructions:

1. Preheat oven to 375°F (190°C) and grease financier molds or muffin tins.
2. Brown the butter in a pan over medium heat, then let it cool.
3. In a bowl, combine almond flour, flour, sugar, and salt.
4. Whisk egg whites until frothy, then add to the dry ingredients.
5. Stir in browned butter and vanilla extract.
6. Pour the batter into the molds and bake for 12-15 minutes until golden and a toothpick comes out clean.

Éclairs

Ingredients:

For the choux pastry:

- 1 cup (120g) all-purpose flour
- 1/2 cup (115g) unsalted butter
- 1 cup (240ml) water
- 1 tsp sugar
- 1/4 tsp salt
- 4 large eggs

For the filling:

- 2 cups (480ml) heavy cream
- 1/4 cup (50g) powdered sugar
- 1 tsp vanilla extract

For the glaze:

- 1 cup (170g) semisweet chocolate, chopped
- 1/2 cup (120ml) heavy cream

Instructions:

1. Preheat oven to 400°F (200°C) and line a baking sheet with parchment paper.
2. In a saucepan, melt butter in water with sugar and salt. Once it boils, add flour and stir until dough forms.
3. Remove from heat and stir in eggs one at a time until smooth.
4. Pipe the dough onto the baking sheet into 4-inch logs. Bake for 20-25 minutes until puffed and golden.
5. For the filling, whip cream with powdered sugar and vanilla until stiff peaks form.
6. For the glaze, melt chocolate and cream together until smooth.
7. Once éclairs are cool, slice open and fill with whipped cream, then dip in chocolate glaze.

Tarte Tatin

Ingredients:

- 6-8 medium apples (preferably Granny Smith or Golden Delicious)
- 1/2 cup (100g) granulated sugar
- 1/4 cup (60g) unsalted butter
- 1 tsp vanilla extract
- 1 sheet puff pastry (store-bought or homemade)

Instructions:

1. Preheat oven to 375°F (190°C).
2. Peel, core, and slice apples into wedges.
3. In a cast-iron skillet, melt butter and sugar over medium heat, stirring until sugar dissolves and caramelizes.
4. Add apples and cook for 10 minutes until they begin to soften.
5. Remove from heat and add vanilla. Place the puff pastry over the apples, tucking in the edges.
6. Bake for 25-30 minutes until the pastry is golden and puffed.
7. Let cool for 5 minutes, then carefully invert the tart onto a plate and serve warm.

Macarons

Ingredients:

- 1 cup (120g) powdered sugar
- 1/2 cup (60g) almond flour
- 3 large egg whites
- 1/4 cup (50g) granulated sugar
- 1 tsp vanilla extract
- 1/4 cup (60g) butter, softened
- 1 cup (120g) powdered sugar (for filling)
- Food coloring (optional)

Instructions:

1. Preheat oven to 300°F (150°C) and line baking sheets with parchment paper.
2. In a food processor, pulse powdered sugar and almond flour until fine. Sift to remove any lumps.
3. Beat egg whites until frothy, then gradually add granulated sugar and beat until stiff peaks form.
4. Gently fold the almond flour mixture into the meringue until smooth.
5. Pipe the mixture onto the baking sheets in 1-inch circles.
6. Let the macarons rest for 30 minutes, then bake for 18-20 minutes until set.
7. For the filling, beat butter and powdered sugar until smooth, then pipe onto half of the cooled macarons and sandwich together.

Pain au Chocolat

Ingredients:

- 2 1/2 cups (310g) all-purpose flour
- 1/4 cup (50g) granulated sugar
- 1 tsp salt
- 1 packet (7g) active dry yeast
- 1 cup (240ml) warm milk
- 1/4 cup (60g) unsalted butter, softened
- 1/2 cup (85g) dark chocolate, chopped

Instructions:

1. Preheat oven to 375°F (190°C) and line a baking sheet with parchment paper.
2. Dissolve yeast and sugar in warm milk and let sit for 5-10 minutes.
3. Mix flour and salt, then add yeast mixture and knead until smooth.
4. Roll dough into a rectangle, fold it over, and refrigerate for 30 minutes.
5. Roll dough out again and cut into 3-inch squares. Place a piece of chocolate in the center of each square and roll up.
6. Let rise for 1 hour, then bake for 15-18 minutes until golden.

Brioche

Ingredients:

- 2 1/2 cups (310g) all-purpose flour
- 1/4 cup (50g) sugar
- 1 tsp salt
- 2 tsp active dry yeast
- 1/2 cup (120ml) warm milk
- 4 large eggs
- 1 cup (225g) unsalted butter, softened

Instructions:

1. Dissolve yeast in warm milk with sugar and let sit for 5-10 minutes.
2. Mix flour and salt in a bowl, then add yeast mixture and eggs. Knead for 10 minutes.
3. Gradually add butter and knead until smooth.
4. Let dough rise for 2 hours until doubled in size.
5. Shape dough into a loaf and bake at 375°F (190°C) for 25-30 minutes until golden.

Clafoutis

Ingredients:

- 1 1/4 cups (160g) all-purpose flour
- 1/2 cup (100g) granulated sugar
- 1 1/2 cups (360ml) whole milk
- 3 large eggs
- 1 tsp vanilla extract
- 1/4 tsp salt
- 1 1/2 cups (200g) pitted cherries (or any fruit)

Instructions:

1. Preheat oven to 350°F (175°C) and grease a baking dish.
2. In a bowl, whisk together flour, sugar, milk, eggs, vanilla, and salt.
3. Pour batter into the prepared dish and arrange cherries evenly.
4. Bake for 35-40 minutes until puffed and golden.
5. Let cool slightly before serving.

Chouquettes

Ingredients:

- 1 cup (120g) all-purpose flour
- 1/2 cup (115g) unsalted butter
- 1 cup (240ml) water
- 1/4 tsp salt
- 1 tsp sugar
- 4 large eggs
- Pearl sugar (for topping)

Instructions:

1. Preheat oven to 375°F (190°C) and line a baking sheet with parchment paper.
2. In a saucepan, melt butter in water with salt and sugar, then bring to a boil.
3. Stir in flour until a dough forms, then let cool slightly.
4. Beat in eggs one at a time until smooth.
5. Pipe dough into small mounds and top with pearl sugar.
6. Bake for 20-25 minutes until puffed and golden.

Canelés

Ingredients:

- 1 1/4 cups (150g) all-purpose flour
- 1 1/2 cups (360ml) whole milk
- 1/2 cup (100g) granulated sugar
- 1/2 tsp vanilla extract
- 1/4 cup (60g) unsalted butter
- 2 large eggs
- 2 tbsp rum

Instructions:

1. Preheat oven to 375°F (190°C) and grease canelé molds.
2. Heat milk, butter, and sugar in a saucepan until the butter melts.
3. In a bowl, whisk flour, eggs, and rum, then pour in the warm milk mixture.
4. Pour batter into molds and bake for 45-50 minutes until golden.
5. Let cool before removing from molds.

Gougères

Ingredients:

- 1 cup (125g) all-purpose flour
- 1/2 cup (115g) unsalted butter
- 1 cup (240ml) water
- 1/2 tsp salt
- 1/4 tsp ground pepper
- 1 cup (100g) grated Gruyère cheese
- 4 large eggs
- 1/2 tsp Dijon mustard (optional)

Instructions:

1. Preheat oven to 375°F (190°C) and line a baking sheet with parchment paper.
2. In a saucepan, melt butter in water with salt, pepper, and mustard (if using).
3. Bring to a boil, then add flour and stir until the dough comes together and pulls away from the sides of the pan.
4. Remove from heat and let cool slightly.
5. Beat in eggs, one at a time, until smooth. Stir in grated cheese.
6. Spoon dough onto the baking sheet, forming small mounds.
7. Bake for 20-25 minutes, until golden and puffed.

Tarte au Citron (Lemon Tart)

Ingredients:

For the crust:

- 1 1/4 cups (160g) all-purpose flour
- 1/4 cup (50g) granulated sugar
- 1/2 cup (115g) unsalted butter, cold and cubed
- 1 egg yolk

For the filling:

- 1 cup (240ml) fresh lemon juice
- Zest of 2 lemons
- 3/4 cup (150g) granulated sugar
- 3 large eggs
- 1/2 cup (120ml) heavy cream

Instructions:

1. Preheat oven to 350°F (175°C).
2. For the crust: Combine flour, sugar, and butter. Blend until crumbly. Add egg yolk and mix until dough forms.
3. Press dough into a tart pan and bake for 10-12 minutes until lightly golden.
4. For the filling: Whisk together lemon juice, zest, sugar, eggs, and cream until smooth.
5. Pour filling into the cooled crust and bake for 20-25 minutes until set. Let cool before serving.

Gâteau Basque

Ingredients:

For the pastry:

- 2 cups (250g) all-purpose flour
- 1/2 cup (100g) sugar
- 1/2 tsp salt
- 1 cup (225g) unsalted butter, softened
- 2 large egg yolks
- 2 tbsp rum

For the filling:

- 1 1/2 cups (375ml) pastry cream (or jam, traditionally cherry or blackcurrant)

Instructions:

1. Preheat oven to 350°F (175°C) and grease a round tart pan.
2. For the pastry: Mix flour, sugar, and salt. Cut in butter until crumbly. Add egg yolks and rum, then mix into dough.
3. Roll out dough and press half into the tart pan. Fill with pastry cream or jam.
4. Roll out the remaining dough and cover the filling.
5. Bake for 35-40 minutes until golden. Let cool before slicing.

Paris-Brest

Ingredients:

For the choux pastry:

- 1 cup (240ml) water
- 1/2 cup (115g) unsalted butter
- 1 cup (125g) all-purpose flour
- 1/4 tsp salt
- 4 large eggs
- 1 tbsp almond flour

For the filling:

- 1 cup (240ml) heavy cream
- 1/4 cup (50g) powdered sugar
- 1/2 tsp vanilla extract
- 1/4 cup (30g) roasted hazelnuts, chopped

Instructions:

1. Preheat oven to 375°F (190°C).
2. For the choux pastry: In a saucepan, bring water, butter, and salt to a boil. Stir in flour until smooth.
3. Remove from heat and add eggs one at a time, mixing until smooth.
4. Pipe dough into a circular shape on a baking sheet. Bake for 30-35 minutes until puffed and golden.
5. For the filling: Whip heavy cream with powdered sugar and vanilla until stiff peaks form.
6. Slice the choux pastry horizontally and fill with whipped cream. Sprinkle with chopped hazelnuts before serving.

Opéra Cake

Ingredients:

For the almond sponge (Biscuit Joconde):

- 1/2 cup (60g) almond flour
- 1/2 cup (60g) powdered sugar
- 3 large eggs
- 1/4 cup (30g) all-purpose flour
- 1/4 cup (60g) unsalted butter, melted

For the coffee syrup:

- 1/2 cup (120ml) brewed coffee
- 1/4 cup (50g) sugar

For the buttercream:

- 1 cup (240g) unsalted butter, softened
- 1/2 cup (100g) granulated sugar
- 2 large egg yolks
- 1/4 cup (60ml) water
- 2 tbsp brewed coffee

For the ganache:

- 1 cup (170g) semisweet chocolate, chopped
- 1/2 cup (120ml) heavy cream

Instructions:

1. Preheat oven to 375°F (190°C).
2. For the sponge: Mix almond flour, powdered sugar, and eggs until smooth. Fold in flour and melted butter. Bake for 10-12 minutes.
3. For the syrup: Combine coffee and sugar, simmer until sugar dissolves.
4. For the buttercream: Whisk egg yolks and water until frothy. In a saucepan, heat sugar and water to 240°F (115°C), then slowly pour over the egg yolks. Beat until thick and creamy. Gradually add softened butter and coffee.
5. For the ganache: Heat cream and pour over chocolate, stirring until smooth.
6. Assemble the cake by layering the sponge, coffee syrup, buttercream, and ganache. Chill for a few hours before serving.

Palmiers

Ingredients:

- 1 sheet puff pastry (store-bought or homemade)
- 1/2 cup (100g) granulated sugar
- 1/2 tsp ground cinnamon

Instructions:

1. Preheat oven to 400°F (200°C) and line a baking sheet with parchment paper.
2. Sprinkle sugar and cinnamon on a clean surface, then roll out the puff pastry over the sugar.
3. Fold the sides of the dough in toward the center, then fold both sides again, creating a long rectangle.
4. Slice dough into 1-inch pieces and place on the baking sheet.
5. Bake for 12-15 minutes until golden and caramelized. Let cool.

Parisian Flan

Ingredients:

For the crust:

- 1 1/4 cups (160g) all-purpose flour
- 1/4 cup (50g) granulated sugar
- 1/2 cup (115g) unsalted butter, cold and cubed
- 1 egg yolk

For the filling:

- 2 cups (480ml) whole milk
- 1/2 cup (100g) granulated sugar
- 1 tsp vanilla extract
- 4 large eggs
- 1/4 cup (30g) all-purpose flour

Instructions:

1. Preheat oven to 350°F (175°C) and grease a tart pan.
2. For the crust: Mix flour, sugar, and butter until crumbly. Add egg yolk and form dough. Press into the tart pan and bake for 12-15 minutes.
3. For the filling: Heat milk and sugar in a saucepan. Whisk eggs and flour in a bowl, then slowly add hot milk mixture to the eggs. Return to the pan and cook until thickened.
4. Pour the filling into the baked crust and bake for 30-35 minutes until set.

Mont-Blanc

Ingredients:

For the meringue:

- 4 large egg whites
- 1 cup (200g) granulated sugar
- 1 tsp vanilla extract

For the chestnut cream:

- 1 can (14 oz/400g) chestnut puree
- 1/2 cup (120ml) heavy cream
- 2 tbsp powdered sugar

Instructions:

1. Preheat oven to 250°F (120°C) and line a baking sheet with parchment paper.
2. For the meringue: Beat egg whites until stiff peaks form, then gradually add sugar and vanilla. Spoon meringue into a piping bag.
3. Pipe the meringue into small rounds and bake for 1-1.5 hours until dry.
4. For the chestnut cream: Whip cream with powdered sugar and fold into chestnut puree.
5. Assemble by layering meringue discs with chestnut cream.

Mille-feuille

Ingredients:

For the puff pastry:

- 2 sheets puff pastry (store-bought or homemade)
- 1 cup (240ml) heavy cream
- 1/4 cup (50g) powdered sugar
- 1 tsp vanilla extract
- 1 tbsp chocolate, melted (optional for decoration)

Instructions:

1. Preheat oven to 400°F (200°C) and line a baking sheet with parchment paper.
2. Bake puff pastry sheets for 15-20 minutes until golden.
3. Whip cream with powdered sugar and vanilla until stiff peaks form.
4. Cut baked puff pastry into rectangles.
5. Layer puff pastry with whipped cream, stacking layers.
6. Drizzle with melted chocolate if desired.

Bûche de Noël (Yule Log)

Ingredients:

For the sponge cake:

- 1 cup (125g) all-purpose flour
- 1 tsp baking powder
- 1/4 tsp salt
- 1/2 cup (115g) granulated sugar
- 4 large eggs
- 1 tsp vanilla extract

For the frosting:

- 1/2 cup (115g) unsalted butter, softened
- 1 1/2 cups (190g) powdered sugar
- 2 tbsp cocoa powder
- 2 tbsp heavy cream
- 1 tsp vanilla extract

Instructions:

1. Preheat oven to 350°F (175°C) and grease a jelly roll pan.
2. For the sponge: Beat eggs and sugar until fluffy, then fold in flour, baking powder, and salt.
3. Bake for 12-15 minutes, then roll the cake while warm in a kitchen towel. Let cool.
4. For the frosting: Beat butter and powdered sugar, then add cocoa, cream, and vanilla.
5. Unroll the cooled cake, spread frosting, and roll it back up.
6. Frost the outside of the cake and decorate with chocolate shavings or powdered sugar.

Madeleines de Commercy

Ingredients:

- 1 cup (125g) all-purpose flour
- 1/2 tsp baking powder
- 1/4 tsp salt
- 1/2 cup (115g) unsalted butter, melted
- 1/2 cup (100g) granulated sugar
- 2 large eggs
- 1 tsp vanilla extract
- Zest of 1 lemon (optional)

Instructions:

1. Preheat oven to 375°F (190°C) and grease madeleine pans.
2. In a bowl, whisk together flour, baking powder, and salt.
3. Beat eggs and sugar until light and fluffy. Stir in melted butter, vanilla, and lemon zest.
4. Gradually add dry ingredients until combined.
5. Spoon batter into madeleine pans and bake for 10-12 minutes until golden.

Quatre-Quarts (French Pound Cake)

Ingredients:

- 1 cup (200g) granulated sugar
- 1 cup (225g) unsalted butter, softened
- 1 cup (125g) all-purpose flour
- 4 large eggs
- 1 tsp vanilla extract
- 1 tsp baking powder
- 1/4 tsp salt

Instructions:

1. Preheat oven to 350°F (175°C) and grease a loaf pan.
2. In a bowl, beat butter and sugar until creamy.
3. Add eggs one at a time, beating well after each addition.
4. Stir in vanilla extract.
5. In a separate bowl, whisk together flour, baking powder, and salt. Gradually add to the wet ingredients and mix until smooth.
6. Pour the batter into the prepared pan and bake for 45-50 minutes, or until a toothpick comes out clean. Let cool before serving.

Gâteau de Mamie (Grandmother's Cake)

Ingredients:

- 2 cups (250g) all-purpose flour
- 1 1/2 tsp baking powder
- 1/4 tsp salt
- 1 cup (200g) sugar
- 1/2 cup (120g) unsalted butter, softened
- 4 large eggs
- 1 tsp vanilla extract
- 1/2 cup (120ml) milk

Instructions:

1. Preheat oven to 350°F (175°C) and grease a cake pan.
2. In a bowl, whisk together flour, baking powder, and salt.
3. In another bowl, beat sugar and butter until creamy.
4. Add eggs one at a time, followed by vanilla extract.
5. Gradually mix in the dry ingredients, alternating with milk, until smooth.
6. Pour the batter into the prepared pan and bake for 30-35 minutes, until golden. Let cool before serving.

Pithiviers

Ingredients:

- 2 sheets puff pastry
- 1 1/2 cups (180g) almond flour
- 3/4 cup (90g) powdered sugar
- 1/4 cup (60g) unsalted butter, softened
- 2 large eggs
- 1 tsp vanilla extract
- 1/4 tsp almond extract (optional)
- 1 egg (for egg wash)

Instructions:

1. Preheat oven to 375°F (190°C) and line a baking sheet with parchment paper.
2. Roll out the puff pastry and cut two circles.
3. In a bowl, mix almond flour, powdered sugar, butter, eggs, and extracts until smooth.
4. Place one pastry circle on the baking sheet, spread the almond mixture, and top with the second circle.
5. Seal the edges and make a small slit in the top. Brush with egg wash.
6. Bake for 25-30 minutes until golden and puffed. Let cool before serving.

Financier au Chocolat

Ingredients:

- 1/2 cup (115g) unsalted butter
- 1 cup (120g) almond flour
- 1/2 cup (60g) all-purpose flour
- 1/2 cup (100g) powdered sugar
- 1/4 cup (50g) granulated sugar
- 4 large egg whites
- 1/4 cup (30g) cocoa powder

Instructions:

1. Preheat oven to 375°F (190°C) and grease financier molds.
2. Brown the butter over medium heat and let cool.
3. In a bowl, whisk together almond flour, all-purpose flour, powdered sugar, granulated sugar, and cocoa powder.
4. Whisk egg whites until frothy, then fold into the dry ingredients.
5. Stir in browned butter until smooth.
6. Pour the batter into molds and bake for 10-12 minutes until golden. Let cool before removing from molds.

Crêpes Suzette

Ingredients:

For the crêpes:

- 1 cup (125g) all-purpose flour
- 2 large eggs
- 1 cup (240ml) milk
- 2 tbsp unsalted butter, melted
- 1 tbsp sugar
- 1 tsp vanilla extract

For the sauce:

- 1/2 cup (120ml) orange juice
- 1/4 cup (60g) unsalted butter
- 1/4 cup (50g) granulated sugar
- 1/4 cup (60ml) orange liqueur (like Grand Marnier)
- 1 tbsp brandy (optional)

Instructions:

1. For the crêpes: In a bowl, whisk together flour, eggs, milk, butter, sugar, and vanilla until smooth.
2. Heat a nonstick skillet and cook crêpes, one at a time, until lightly golden on both sides. Set aside.
3. For the sauce: In a pan, melt butter and sugar over medium heat, then add orange juice and bring to a simmer.
4. Add orange liqueur and brandy, then ignite the alcohol to flambé (optional).
5. Fold the crêpes into quarters and place in the sauce. Let them soak for 1-2 minutes.
6. Serve the crêpes with the sauce, garnished with orange zest.

Mousse au Chocolat

Ingredients:

- 8 oz (225g) semisweet or bittersweet chocolate, chopped
- 1 cup (240ml) heavy cream
- 2 tbsp sugar
- 3 large egg whites
- 2 tbsp granulated sugar

Instructions:

1. Melt chocolate in a heatproof bowl over simmering water or in the microwave.
2. Whip heavy cream with sugar until stiff peaks form.
3. Beat egg whites with granulated sugar until stiff peaks form.
4. Gently fold the melted chocolate into the whipped cream, then fold in the egg whites until smooth.
5. Spoon the mousse into serving glasses and refrigerate for 2-3 hours before serving.

Poached Pears in Red Wine

Ingredients:

- 4 pears, peeled and cored
- 2 cups (480ml) red wine
- 1/2 cup (100g) granulated sugar
- 1 cinnamon stick
- 2-3 cloves
- 1 strip lemon peel

Instructions:

1. In a saucepan, combine red wine, sugar, cinnamon stick, cloves, and lemon peel.
2. Add pears and simmer for 20-30 minutes, turning occasionally, until pears are tender.
3. Remove pears and reduce the liquid by half to form a syrup.
4. Serve the pears with the syrup poured over them.

Tartelette aux Fruits (Fruit Tartlets)

Ingredients:

For the crust:

- 1 1/4 cups (160g) all-purpose flour
- 1/4 cup (50g) sugar
- 1/2 cup (115g) unsalted butter, cold and cubed
- 1 egg yolk

For the filling:

- 1/2 cup (120ml) heavy cream
- 1/2 cup (120ml) milk
- 1/4 cup (50g) sugar
- 2 large egg yolks
- 1 tsp vanilla extract

For the topping:

- Assorted fresh fruits (berries, kiwi, etc.)

Instructions:

1. Preheat oven to 350°F (175°C) and grease small tart pans.
2. For the crust: Mix flour, sugar, and butter until crumbly. Add egg yolk and form dough. Press into tart pans and bake for 12-15 minutes.
3. For the filling: Heat cream and milk in a saucepan. In a bowl, whisk sugar and egg yolks. Gradually add hot milk mixture to eggs, then return to the pan and cook until thickened.
4. Pour the filling into cooled tart shells and top with fresh fruit.

Choux à la Crème (Cream Puffs)

Ingredients:

For the choux pastry:

- 1 cup (240ml) water
- 1/2 cup (115g) unsalted butter
- 1 cup (125g) all-purpose flour
- 1/4 tsp salt
- 4 large eggs

For the filling:

- 1 cup (240ml) heavy cream
- 2 tbsp powdered sugar
- 1 tsp vanilla extract

Instructions:

1. Preheat oven to 375°F (190°C) and line a baking sheet with parchment paper.
2. For the choux pastry: Boil water, butter, and salt in a saucepan. Stir in flour until a dough forms.
3. Remove from heat and add eggs, one at a time, mixing until smooth.
4. Pipe dough onto the baking sheet in small mounds. Bake for 20-25 minutes until puffed and golden.
5. For the filling: Whip heavy cream with powdered sugar and vanilla until stiff peaks form.
6. Slice the cream puffs open, fill with whipped cream, and serve.

Sablés

Ingredients:

- 1 1/2 cups (190g) all-purpose flour
- 1/2 cup (100g) granulated sugar
- 1/2 tsp vanilla extract
- 1/4 tsp salt
- 1 cup (225g) unsalted butter, softened

Instructions:

1. Preheat oven to 350°F (175°C) and line a baking sheet with parchment paper.
2. Beat butter and sugar until smooth. Add vanilla extract and salt.
3. Gradually add flour and mix until smooth.
4. Roll dough into a log, slice into rounds, and place on the baking sheet.
5. Bake for 10-12 minutes until golden.

Tarte Bourdaloue

Ingredients:

For the crust:

- 1 1/4 cups (160g) all-purpose flour
- 1/4 cup (50g) sugar
- 1/2 cup (115g) unsalted butter, cold and cubed
- 1 egg yolk

For the filling:

- 1 1/4 cups (150g) almond cream (made with almond flour, butter, sugar, and egg)
- 1/2 cup (80g) canned pears, drained and sliced
- 1 tbsp sliced almonds

Instructions:

1. Preheat oven to 350°F (175°C) and grease a tart pan.
2. For the crust: Mix flour, sugar, and butter until crumbly. Add egg yolk and form dough. Press into the tart pan and bake for 10-12 minutes.
3. Spread almond cream over the baked crust.
4. Arrange pear slices on top of the almond cream and sprinkle with sliced almonds.
5. Bake for 30-35 minutes until set and golden.

Caramelized Apple Cake

Ingredients:

For the caramelized apples:

- 4 medium apples, peeled, cored, and sliced
- 1/2 cup (100g) granulated sugar
- 2 tbsp unsalted butter

For the cake:

- 1 1/2 cups (190g) all-purpose flour
- 1 1/2 tsp baking powder
- 1/4 tsp salt
- 1/2 cup (115g) unsalted butter, softened
- 1 cup (200g) granulated sugar
- 2 large eggs
- 1 tsp vanilla extract
- 1/2 cup (120ml) milk

Instructions:

1. Preheat oven to 350°F (175°C) and grease a 9-inch round cake pan.
2. For the caramelized apples: In a pan, melt sugar over medium heat until it turns golden. Add butter and sliced apples, cooking for 5-7 minutes until caramelized.
3. For the cake: Beat butter and sugar until fluffy, then add eggs and vanilla. Gradually add dry ingredients, alternating with milk.
4. Pour batter into the pan, arrange caramelized apples on top, and bake for 35-40 minutes until golden.

Gâteau Saint-Honoré

Ingredients:

For the puff pastry base:

- 1 sheet puff pastry (store-bought or homemade)

For the choux pastry:

- 1 cup (240ml) water
- 1/2 cup (115g) unsalted butter
- 1 cup (125g) all-purpose flour
- 1/4 tsp salt
- 4 large eggs

For the crème chiboust:

- 1 1/2 cups (360ml) milk
- 1/2 cup (100g) sugar
- 4 large egg yolks
- 1 tbsp cornstarch
- 1/2 tsp vanilla extract
- 3 large egg whites
- 1/4 cup (50g) sugar

Instructions:

1. Preheat oven to 375°F (190°C) and line a baking sheet with parchment paper.
2. For the puff pastry: Bake puff pastry for 10-12 minutes until golden, then cut into a circle to form the base.
3. For the choux pastry: In a saucepan, melt butter in water with salt. Stir in flour until dough forms. Let cool slightly, then add eggs one at a time.
4. Pipe choux pastry into small puffs and bake for 20 minutes until puffed and golden.
5. For the crème chiboust: Heat milk and sugar. Whisk egg yolks and cornstarch, then slowly add the hot milk mixture. Cook until thickened.
6. Whip egg whites with sugar until stiff peaks form, then fold into the cream mixture.
7. Assemble by filling choux puffs with cream and arranging them on the puff pastry base.

Pain d'Épices (Spiced Cake)

Ingredients:

- 2 cups (250g) all-purpose flour
- 1 tsp baking powder
- 1 tsp ground cinnamon
- 1/2 tsp ground ginger
- 1/4 tsp ground cloves
- 1/4 tsp salt
- 3/4 cup (150g) honey
- 1/4 cup (50g) brown sugar
- 1/2 cup (120ml) milk
- 2 large eggs

Instructions:

1. Preheat oven to 350°F (175°C) and grease a loaf pan.
2. In a bowl, whisk together flour, baking powder, and spices.
3. In another bowl, mix honey, brown sugar, milk, and eggs.
4. Gradually add dry ingredients to wet ingredients, stirring until smooth.
5. Pour the batter into the pan and bake for 40-45 minutes until a toothpick comes out clean. Let cool before serving.

Dacquoise

Ingredients:

For the meringue:

- 2 1/2 cups (300g) powdered sugar
- 1 cup (100g) almond flour
- 6 large egg whites
- 1/2 tsp cream of tartar

For the filling:

- 1 1/2 cups (360ml) heavy cream
- 1/4 cup (50g) powdered sugar
- 1 tsp vanilla extract

Instructions:

1. Preheat oven to 300°F (150°C) and line baking sheets with parchment paper.
2. For the meringue: Beat egg whites with cream of tartar until stiff peaks form. Gradually add powdered sugar and almond flour.
3. Spoon meringue into circles or layers on the parchment paper and bake for 1-1.5 hours until dry and crisp.
4. For the filling: Whip cream with powdered sugar and vanilla until stiff peaks form.
5. Once the meringue layers cool, layer them with whipped cream and serve.

Parisian Macarons with Fruit Filling

Ingredients:

For the macaron shells:

- 1 1/4 cups (150g) powdered sugar
- 1 cup (120g) almond flour
- 3 large egg whites
- 1/4 cup (50g) granulated sugar
- 1/2 tsp vanilla extract

For the fruit filling:

- 1/2 cup (100g) fruit puree (e.g., raspberry, strawberry)
- 1/2 cup (120ml) heavy cream
- 1/4 cup (50g) powdered sugar

Instructions:

1. Preheat oven to 300°F (150°C) and line baking sheets with parchment paper.
2. For the macaron shells: Sift powdered sugar and almond flour together. Beat egg whites until stiff peaks form, then gradually add granulated sugar. Fold in the dry ingredients.
3. Pipe the macaron mixture onto the parchment paper in small circles. Let them rest for 30 minutes.
4. Bake for 15-20 minutes, then let cool.
5. For the filling: Whip heavy cream with powdered sugar, then fold in fruit puree.
6. Assemble the macarons by filling them with the fruit cream.

Flan Pâtissier (French Custard Tart)

Ingredients:

For the crust:

- 1 1/4 cups (160g) all-purpose flour
- 1/4 cup (50g) granulated sugar
- 1/2 cup (115g) unsalted butter, cold and cubed
- 1 egg yolk

For the filling:

- 2 cups (480ml) whole milk
- 1/2 cup (100g) granulated sugar
- 4 large egg yolks
- 2 tbsp cornstarch
- 1 tsp vanilla extract

Instructions:

1. Preheat oven to 350°F (175°C) and grease a tart pan.
2. For the crust: Mix flour, sugar, and butter until crumbly. Add egg yolk and form dough. Press into the tart pan and bake for 12-15 minutes.
3. For the filling: Heat milk and sugar in a saucepan. In a bowl, whisk egg yolks and cornstarch. Gradually add the hot milk mixture to the eggs. Return to the pan and cook until thickened.
4. Pour filling into the baked crust and bake for 20-25 minutes. Let cool before serving.

Gâteau au Yaourt (Yogurt Cake)

Ingredients:

- 1 1/2 cups (190g) all-purpose flour
- 1 tsp baking powder
- 1/4 tsp salt
- 1 cup (240g) plain yogurt
- 1 cup (200g) granulated sugar
- 1/2 cup (120ml) vegetable oil
- 3 large eggs
- 1 tsp vanilla extract

Instructions:

1. Preheat oven to 350°F (175°C) and grease a cake pan.
2. In a bowl, whisk together flour, baking powder, and salt.
3. In another bowl, mix yogurt, sugar, oil, eggs, and vanilla.
4. Gradually add dry ingredients to wet ingredients and stir until smooth.
5. Pour batter into the pan and bake for 30-35 minutes until golden. Let cool before serving.

Tartelette au Chocolat

Ingredients:

For the crust:

- 1 1/4 cups (160g) all-purpose flour
- 1/4 cup (50g) granulated sugar
- 1/2 cup (115g) unsalted butter, cold and cubed
- 1 egg yolk

For the filling:

- 1 cup (240ml) heavy cream
- 8 oz (225g) semisweet chocolate, chopped
- 1 tsp vanilla extract

Instructions:

1. Preheat oven to 350°F (175°C) and grease tartlet pans.
2. For the crust: Mix flour, sugar, and butter until crumbly. Add egg yolk and form dough. Press into tartlet pans and bake for 10-12 minutes.
3. For the filling: Heat cream and pour over chopped chocolate. Stir until smooth and add vanilla.
4. Pour the chocolate filling into cooled crusts and refrigerate for 2-3 hours until set.

Framboisier (Raspberry Cake)

Ingredients:

- 1 1/2 cups (190g) all-purpose flour
- 1/2 tsp baking powder
- 1/4 tsp salt
- 1 cup (200g) granulated sugar
- 4 large eggs
- 1/2 cup (120ml) milk
- 1 tsp vanilla extract
- 1 1/2 cups (150g) fresh raspberries

For the filling:

- 1 1/2 cups (360ml) whipped cream
- 1 tbsp powdered sugar

Instructions:

1. Preheat oven to 350°F (175°C) and grease a round cake pan.
2. Mix flour, baking powder, and salt.
3. Beat eggs and sugar until fluffy, then gradually add dry ingredients.
4. Add milk and vanilla extract, mixing until smooth.
5. Bake for 25-30 minutes until golden. Let cool.
6. For the filling: Whip cream with powdered sugar until stiff.
7. Slice the cake, fill with whipped cream, and layer raspberries on top.

Palet Breton

Ingredients:

- 1 1/4 cups (160g) all-purpose flour
- 1/4 cup (50g) granulated sugar
- 1/4 tsp salt
- 1/2 cup (115g) unsalted butter, softened
- 2 large egg yolks
- 1/2 tsp vanilla extract

Instructions:

1. Preheat oven to 350°F (175°C) and line a baking sheet with parchment paper.
2. Mix flour, sugar, and salt. Add butter and mix until crumbly.
3. Add egg yolks and vanilla, then form dough.
4. Roll dough into a log, slice into rounds, and place on the baking sheet.
5. Bake for 10-12 minutes until golden.

Crêpes with Sugar

Ingredients:

- 1 cup (125g) all-purpose flour
- 1 1/2 cups (360ml) milk
- 2 large eggs
- 2 tbsp melted butter
- 1/4 tsp salt
- Granulated sugar, for sprinkling

Instructions:

1. In a bowl, whisk together flour, milk, eggs, butter, and salt.
2. Heat a nonstick skillet over medium heat and lightly grease it.
3. Pour in a small amount of batter, swirling to coat the bottom of the skillet.
4. Cook for 1-2 minutes until the edges lift, then flip and cook for another minute.
5. Serve with a sprinkle of sugar on top.

Nougat

Ingredients:

- 2 cups (400g) granulated sugar
- 1/2 cup (120ml) honey
- 1/4 cup (60ml) water
- 2 large egg whites
- 1 1/2 cups (200g) mixed nuts (almonds, hazelnuts, etc.)
- 1 tsp vanilla extract
- 1/4 tsp salt

Instructions:

1. Line a baking pan with parchment paper.
2. In a saucepan, combine sugar, honey, and water, then bring to a simmer until the syrup reaches 250°F (120°C).
3. In a separate bowl, whip egg whites with salt until stiff peaks form.
4. Gradually pour the hot syrup into the egg whites while beating continuously.
5. Fold in mixed nuts and vanilla extract.
6. Pour the mixture into the prepared pan, spreading evenly.
7. Let cool for several hours or overnight, then cut into squares and serve.

Meringues

Ingredients:

- 4 large egg whites
- 1 cup (200g) granulated sugar
- 1 tsp vanilla extract
- 1/4 tsp cream of tartar

Instructions:

1. Preheat oven to 225°F (110°C) and line a baking sheet with parchment paper.
2. Beat egg whites with cream of tartar until soft peaks form.
3. Gradually add sugar, a spoonful at a time, and continue beating until stiff peaks form.
4. Stir in vanilla extract.
5. Spoon or pipe meringue onto the baking sheet in small mounds.
6. Bake for 1-1.5 hours until crisp and golden. Let cool before serving.

Biscuit Rose de Reims

Ingredients:

- 2 cups (250g) all-purpose flour
- 1 cup (200g) granulated sugar
- 1 tsp baking powder
- 1/4 tsp salt
- 2 large eggs
- 1/2 tsp vanilla extract
- 1/4 cup (60ml) milk
- 1/4 cup (50g) cornstarch
- 1/4 cup (50g) powdered sugar (for dusting)

Instructions:

1. Preheat oven to 350°F (175°C) and line a baking sheet with parchment paper.
2. In a bowl, whisk together flour, sugar, baking powder, salt, and cornstarch.
3. In another bowl, beat eggs and vanilla until light and fluffy.
4. Gradually add the dry ingredients, alternating with milk, and mix until smooth.
5. Spoon the batter into piping bags and pipe finger-shaped biscuits onto the baking sheet.
6. Bake for 10-12 minutes until lightly golden. Let cool.
7. Dust with powdered sugar before serving.

Tarte Normande

Ingredients:

For the crust:

- 1 1/4 cups (160g) all-purpose flour
- 1/4 cup (50g) granulated sugar
- 1/2 cup (115g) unsalted butter, cold and cubed
- 1 egg yolk

For the filling:

- 3 large apples, peeled, cored, and sliced
- 1/2 cup (100g) granulated sugar
- 1/2 cup (120ml) heavy cream
- 2 large eggs
- 1 tsp vanilla extract
- 1/4 tsp ground cinnamon

Instructions:

1. Preheat oven to 375°F (190°C) and grease a tart pan.
2. For the crust: Mix flour, sugar, and butter until crumbly. Add egg yolk and form dough. Press into tart pan and bake for 10-12 minutes.
3. For the filling: Whisk together sugar, cream, eggs, vanilla, and cinnamon until smooth.
4. Arrange apple slices over the partially baked crust, then pour filling over the apples.
5. Bake for 30-35 minutes until set and golden. Let cool before serving.

Gâteau de Voyage

Ingredients:

- 2 1/2 cups (310g) all-purpose flour
- 1 1/2 tsp baking powder
- 1/2 tsp salt
- 1/2 cup (115g) unsalted butter, softened
- 1 cup (200g) granulated sugar
- 4 large eggs
- 1 tsp vanilla extract
- 1/2 cup (120ml) milk
- 1/4 cup (50g) fruit jam (optional, for filling)

Instructions:

1. Preheat oven to 350°F (175°C) and grease a loaf pan.
2. In a bowl, whisk together flour, baking powder, and salt.
3. Beat butter and sugar until fluffy, then add eggs one at a time.
4. Gradually add dry ingredients, alternating with milk.
5. Pour the batter into the prepared pan and bake for 40-45 minutes, until a toothpick comes out clean.
6. Optionally, slice the cake and spread fruit jam between layers for a delightful surprise. Let cool before serving.

Sablé Breton

Ingredients:

- 1 1/4 cups (160g) all-purpose flour
- 1/2 cup (100g) granulated sugar
- 1/4 tsp salt
- 1/2 cup (115g) unsalted butter, softened
- 3 large egg yolks
- 1 tsp vanilla extract
- 1 tbsp milk

Instructions:

1. Preheat oven to 350°F (175°C) and line a baking sheet with parchment paper.
2. Mix flour, sugar, and salt in a bowl.
3. Add butter, egg yolks, vanilla, and milk, and mix until smooth.
4. Roll the dough out to about 1/4 inch thick and cut into shapes (traditionally round).
5. Bake for 12-15 minutes until golden brown. Let cool before serving.

www.ingramcontent.com/pod-product-compliance
Lightning Source LLC
LaVergne TN
LVHW081337060526
838201LV00055B/2706